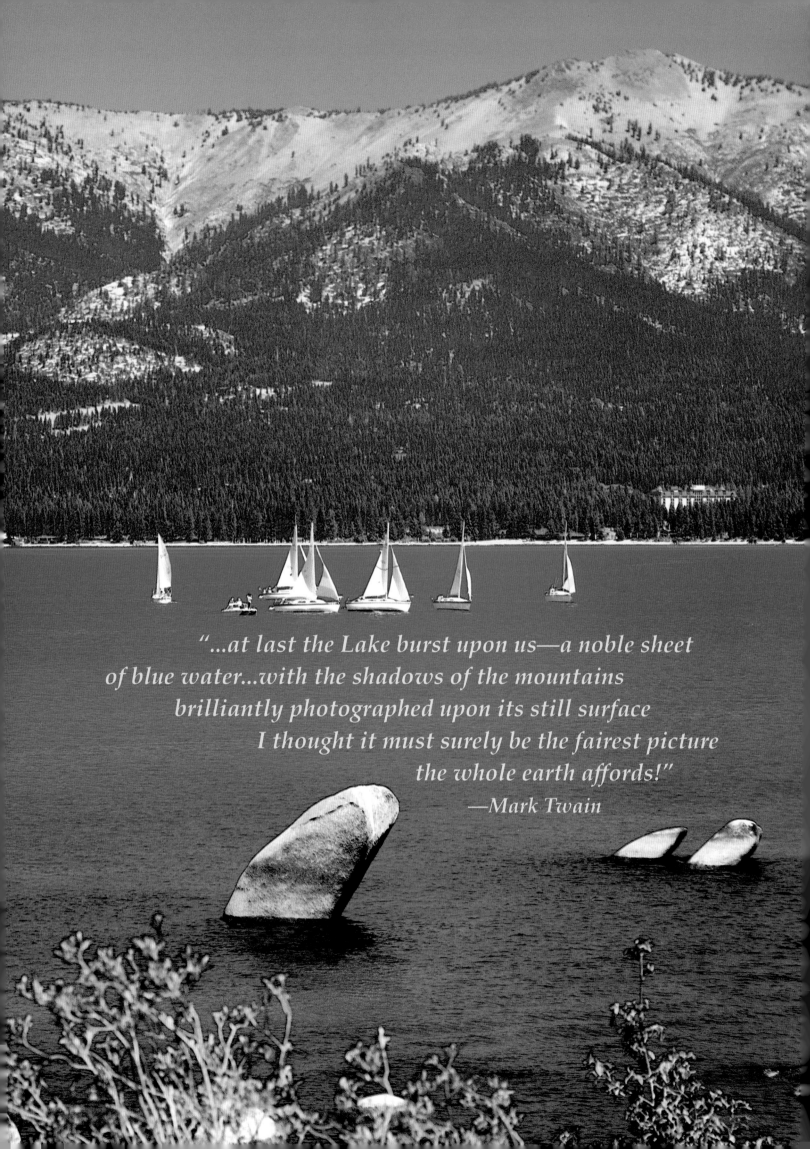

"...at last the Lake burst upon us—a noble sheet
of blue water...with the shadows of the mountains
brilliantly photographed upon its still surface
I thought it must surely be the fairest picture
the whole earth affords!"
—Mark Twain

▲ **Lake Tahoe,** *shared by California and Nevada, is located 100 miles east of Sacramento and 35 miles southwest of Reno, high in the Sierra Nevada.*

Front and back covers: Emerald Bay—the most spectacular and popular inlet of Lake Tahoe; Inside front cover: D. L. Bliss State Park, photos by Gail Bandini. Page 1: Skier at Alpine Meadows, photo by Larry Prosor. Pages 2/3: Sailboats glide past a rocky shoreline, photo by Ed Cooper. Pages 4/5: Pines frame Lake Tahoe at D. L. Bliss State Park, photo by George Wuerthner. Mark Twain visited this virtually uninhabited wilderness in 1861.

Edited by Mary L. Van Camp.
Book design by K. C. DenDooven.

Second Printing, 1997

Destination - LAKE TAHOE: The Story Behind the Scenery
© 1994 KC PUBLICATIONS, INC.

"The Story Behind the Scenery"; "in pictures... The Continuing Story'
the parallelogram forms and colors within are registered
in the U.S. Patent and Trademark Office.

LC 94-78129. ISBN 0-88714-088-2.

Destination
LAKE TAHOE
THE STORY BEHIND THE SCENERY®

by Stanley W. Paher

A native Nevadan, Stanley Paher has written and published over a dozen books on the Southwestern desert and its ghost towns. He is also the author of *Scotty's Castle* in the "Story Behind the Scenery" series. Currently living in Reno, Paher has first-hand knowledge of and feeling for the brilliant gem of nature that is Lake Tahoe.

Until modern times the peaceful lake lay mostly undisturbed by man, except for annual summertime visits by area Washoe Indians.

The Discovery of Lake Tahoe

Hemmed in by the majestic, rocky, tree-studded alpine mountains of the rugged Sierra Nevada, Lake Tahoe at a 6,223-foot altitude is among the world's most remarkable fresh-water lakes. Three score delightfully cool snow-fed streams flow into the oval-shaped basin, annually replenishing and renewing the crystal-cool waters of this "lake in the sky." Little wonder, then, that for decades on end various artists, poets, writers, and journalists have praised Lake Tahoe's versatile beauty and secluded charm.

From towering snowy peaks on every side of this 22-mile-long by 12-mile-wide lake, bold granite masses and thickly studded evergreen forests gradually descend toward the deep-blue waters, blending abruptly with flat, grassy meadows which recede from the vast sandy stretches of shoreline. Not

◀ **The sharp contrast** ▶ of seasons is apparent in these aerial views. In summer, forested mountains rise abruptly above Heavenly Valley and Stateline's casino district and Edgewood Golf Course. Tahoe's turquoise summer waters turn to deep blue in winter owing to the purity, great water depths, and the cloudless sky. A popular destination in winter, Heavenly Valley ski area—among the nation's largest—straddles the California-Nevada state line.

LARRY PROSOR

An intrepid ▶ hiker descends a rocky slope in Shirley Canyon, immediately northwest of Lake Tahoe. These icy waters eventually join the Truckee River, Tahoe's only outlet. The numerous trails in Tahoe Basin offer alternatives for every degree of hiking skill.

LARRY PROSOR

surprisingly, such a versatile natural treasure is the site of almost every kind of winter and summer outdoor sports, and indoor recreation.

Straddling the California-Nevada state line, Lake Tahoe also serves the useful function of a natural reservoir and water supply for several eastern California communities as well as towns and ranches of western Nevada. The Truckee River lifeline originates on the northwest shore, then flows northward toward the town of Truckee and eastward through urban Reno and Sparks before it empties into Pyramid Lake, a land-locked desert lake only 75 miles northeast of the river's origin. Just before the water reaches Pyramid, diversion ditches of the Newlands Reclamation Project send the valuable water to scores of ranches and farms located on inland Nevada deserts.

Until modern times the peaceful lake lay mostly undisturbed by man, except for seasonal

summertime visits by Washoe Indians entering the Tahoe Basin in search of quail, grouse, trout, and other game and fish. They built no permanent dwellings. Then in the winter of 1844, the 39-man party of explorer John C. Fremont entered the present western Nevada, discovering Pyramid Lake before venturing into the foothills and eastern slopes of the Sierra Nevada. At a point near Stevens Peak and Red Mountain, Fremont and his cartographer, Charles Preuss, climbed a high peak and sighted the large alpine lake 16 miles to the north. They named it Bonpland, but later designations on early maps after 1853 called it Lake Bigler or Mountain Lake.

Bypassing a visit to the mirror-like water, the Fremont expedition crossed the Sierra westward through a pass named after its scout, Kit Carson. All the while, the Americans had been intruding upon Mexico's "Alta California," mostly uninhabited except along the Pacific coastal regions

△ *From a vantage point high in the Sierra Nevada above Lake Tahoe, a family of hikers* enjoys virtually the same view as that witnessed by the John C. Fremont exploration party in 1844. By 1860, numerous silver seekers rushed past Tahoe's rich blue waters to Virginia City, Nevada Territory, 30 miles east.

where a string of Spanish missions and large ranchos thrived under the governorship of Monterey, a village south of San Francisco. Two years later, in 1846, various skirmishes broke out between Americans and Mexicans in various parts of the Southwest, but Tahoe remained entirely unaffected. In 1848 this area was annexed to the western United States, and following the creation of California in 1850, roughly two-thirds of the mountain lake ultimately became part of

the new state when an 1855 boundary survey determined the state's eastern boundary.

GOLD DISCOVERED

Early in 1848 flake gold was discovered on the South Fork of the American River at Coloma, 50 miles west in the foothills of the Sierra Nevada, to the west, and during the next year the famous great gold rush to "Californy" developed. Within a few years tens of thousands of

On old U.S. ▶
Highway 40, west of the town of Truckee, the Donner Spitz Hutte bed and breakfast lodge sits on Donner Summit. This high mountain hotel blends the Old World spirit of the Alps with the contemporary style of California's Sierra.

would-be miners, as well as farmers, businessmen, and various tradesmen migrated west, traversing the Sierra Nevada on the main California Trail used by the ill-fated Donner Party (15 miles north of Tahoe), the Carson Pass route (9 miles to the south), and four other major trails. None of these approached the Tahoe Basin, for it was regarded as a mere barrier to a successful ending of a long westward journey by the argonauts. Lake Tahoe would still be visited from spring to fall only by the area Washoes.

Through the early 1850s, the wild rush of westbound fortune seekers and adventurers continued to California unabated, and Tahoe remained undisturbed. But by mid-decade the traffic slowed when the mother lode's gold camps began to experience dull times. Twenty-five miles east of Tahoe, in Cold Canyon or "Washoe," a vanguard of placer miners was recovering gold in streambed gravel, but in the spring of 1859 a dramatic change of events occurred. Bluish silver quartz was discovered at the head of the canyon near present-day Virginia City. The cry in the worked-out California mining

camps was "Silver! Silver in Washoe!" Thousands of pedestrians with backpacks stuffed with food and tools now rushed *eastward* to the new find to stake out their mining claims; but still Tahoe itself was ignored, lightly esteemed as a place of settlement or opportunity.

During 1860-61 the famous lean Pony Express riders skirted the south end of the lake where two change stations for horses were maintained. The overland stage and telegraph lines also were placed along what is now roughly U.S. 50 in California. But still it was the eastbound California silver seekers who created the most traffic on what soon became known as the "Placerville Route" to Nevada. From Placerville, also known as "Hangtown," the well-beaten road led past Meyers Station as it approached Lake Tahoe, Sierra House, Friday's, and then northward along the lake's east side to Glenbrook. Thereafter, the road veered eastward to Virginia City and the Comstock Lode, in all, a two- to three-week trip on foot from Hangtown. For a San Franciscan in a horse-drawn stage, however, it took only 36 hours to travel all the

A wooden emigrant ▷ wagon appropriately laden with snow memorializes the Donner party's winter camp of 1846. An early fall storm prevented the Donner wagon train from crossing the high Sierra Nevada to their eventual destination, the lush valleys of northern California.

ED COOPER

way to the new promised land in 1863, via the south Tahoe stations.

Glenbrook, particularly, was more than a roadhouse stop for stages and the silver-mad crowd of would-be Comstockers. The new silver camp needed timber for houses, business buildings, and especially for the mines' underground square-set supports. Mine owners would soon look covetously to the magnificent stands of timber in the Tahoe basin, and Glenbrook's Captain Pray built a sawmill on the lake in the summer of

1861. It joined a small water-powered mill in operation in Lake Valley, on the west side. Soon saw logs jammed the southwest corner of Glenbrook Bay and in 1863 horse-drawn wagons carried the cut lumber eastward via Spooner's Summit to the Comstock. By 1864, Pray also was operating a small excursion steamer, the *Governor Blaisdel*, to provide recreation on the lake. These pioneer efforts were but precursors to further lumber and steamship operations on Lake Tahoe.

◁ *Thousands of* tourists annually visit Donner Memorial State Park in California, where museum exhibits and programs explain the Sierra Nevada's natural history and also depict the ordeal of the westbound Donner emigrant party, trapped for weeks near this site.

Lake Tahoe's Potential Realized

In the spring of 1861, isolated Lake Tahoe, shared by California and the new territory of Nevada, stood by as Abraham Lincoln desperately tried to hold the nation together before Civil War broke out in the East. The President sent Orion Clemens west to serve as secretary of the two-month-old territory, accompanied by his brother, Sam, better known as Mark Twain. Once in Carson City, the territorial capital, the enthusiastic, spirited future humorist's first goal was to backpack westward into Lake Bigler (Tahoe).

In August, Twain and a friend were overpowered by the lake's glorious transparent surface and the fastnesses of the tree-studded surrounding mountains. They had entered the vast oval basin at a point three miles north of the sawmill at Glenbrook, the largest

◀ **Mountain breezes** *slightly wrinkle "Big Blue's" clear, azure waters, while an early fall snow dusts the distant Carson Range. Here is Tahoe stripped to essentials—the ultimate in simplicity and beauty.*

LARRY PROSOR

A *kayak is seemingly* ▶ *suspended in air above the wondrous, crystal surface of the freshwater pool, Tahoe. The shoreline waters afford views of Tahoe's rocky floor to great depths.*

enterprise in that wilderness. The tranquil, deep-blue lake mirrored the lofty Sierra Nevada peaks to the west.

Besides staking out a rich 300-acre timber claim north of Glenbrook by nailing a notice to a pine tree, the two men also ventured onto the lake in a small borrowed boat. At depths of only about 30 feet the lake bottom seemed perfectly clear and they felt as though the boat was floating in the air! "Where it was 80 feet deep, every little pebble was distinct, every speckled trout, every hand's breath of sand." Boulders climbed to the lake's surface only to descend again, not harming the boat. "Down through the transparency of these great depths, the water was not merely transparent but dazzlingly so, brilliantly so....All objects seen through it had a bright, strong vividness, not only of outline but of every minute detail, which they would not have had seen through the same depths of atmosphere."

Soon after returning to his east-shore camp, Twain inadvertently started a small forest fire, and so the men abandoned their wood ranch. Also, they had not completely fenced in the land to perfect their claim. Years later, in his book *Roughing It*, Twain recalled the exhilarating days camping out and the bracing mountain air which to him almost seemed to possess curative qualities. "Three months of camp life on Lake Tahoe would restore an Egyptian mummy to his pristine vigor, and give him an appetite like an alligator. I do not mean the oldest and driest mummies, of course, but the fresher ones...."

Twain returned to Carson City in September 1861, leaving the mountain lake to developers with business judgment and the constant horde of eastbound transients skirting the lake's south shore bound for the silver ledges below Virginia City. Along the south shore were inns, corrals, and small stores catering to these thousands afoot with backpacks and pack animals with other provisions, hundreds of horsemen, and still more comfortably seated in stagecoaches. The road-houses needed food for man and beast, and $250-a-ton hand-bailed hay was delivered by two-master schooners from small ranches on the lake's west shore. Teamsters hauled in vegetables and other foods from area truck farms. One enterprising rancher drove about 500 turkeys along the route to the delight of many Nevadans.

Nestled *in a backdrop of a* ▷
conifer forest and rugged mountain ranges, Sand Harbor is but one of many picturesque inlets around Lake Tahoe. In contrast with the hordes of summer swimmers who invade the white, sandy beaches, wintertime is highlighted by translucent blue waters meeting shoreline boulders capped by snow.

NAMING THE LAKE

About this same time there was controversy about the name of the lake. John C. Fremont's names Mountain Lake and Lake Bonpland never saw much popular use, and in 1852 the California legislature designated it Lake Bigler after the present sitting Democratic governor. But with the political mood of the country moving in another direction in the early 1860s, triumphant Republicanism rechristened these exquisite surroundings Tahoe, an Indian word signifying "snow water."

This name came from the research of explorer and ethnologist Dr. Henry De Groot, who compiled a vocabulary of area Indian tribe words. Only three years earlier De Groot had published the first book which described the months-old silver mines of Virginia City and the agricultural resources, climate, and travel routes east of the Sierra, along with a valuable map properly show-

KEN MC KOWEN

ing the main trails between California and western Nevada all bypassing "Lake Bigler" (then the official name).

De Groot soon suggested that *tah-oo-ee*, which meant snow, and *tah-oo*, meaning water, were more descriptive of the cool mountain lake. Others have offered various opinions as to the origins of the lake's name, even one explanation that the lake's name came from the Spanish *tajo*, which generally means a deep water-filled

◄ **The Phipps cabin at Sugar Pine Point** dates back to 1872, when General Phipps, an old Indian fighter, established a foothold in the area by erecting this structure and damming up the mouth of a nearby creek in which to keep fish.

chasm, or cut. Through common usage, the name Tahoe caught on almost immediately, but no federal or state action was taken to relieve map publishers of using Lake Bigler. Though uttered by the Indians as "Tah-oo," palefaces pronounced it "Ta-hoe," and it was generally thus after 1863.

All through the Civil War years of 1861-1865, the lake's only permanent community was Glenbrook, where Captain Pray's 1861 sawmill was joined by several others on Clear Creek, in the Carson Range immediately east of the lake and ten miles closer to Virginia City's Comstock mines. Pray also built a new $20,000 sawmill at Glenbrook. Two other men built the Monitor Mill at Glenbrook in 1863, bringing the total number of mills in the vicinity to at least six.

Besides the sawmills, Glenbrook boasted a resort and spa to provide boating and other recre-

Besides primitive pleasure resorts, Lake Tahoe possessed other assets that the outside world coveted. Throughout the 19th-century Comstock silver boom at Virginia City the lake was a prime source for the town's timber and water, and its confident, high-living entrepreneurs exploited these ▼ assets aggressively. Thus, Virginia City left an indelible impress on the Tahoe Basin.

ation for wealthier Virginia City mining and business people weary of mine blasts and the Comstock's fast pace. Here the aristocracy could enjoy the Glenbrook House's fare and entertainment, the surrounding meadows, and boating and swimming in the lake. At this time, the famous stagecoach king, Ben Holladay, maintained a rustic cottage at Emerald Bay, the first of many private vacation sites to be developed in the basin.

On the northwest shore, where the Truckee River begins its flow from Lake Tahoe, a cluster of wooden dwellings built in the mid-1860s became Tahoe City, which in 1867 had a three-year-old hotel, saloons, a store, and a dozen small craft at anchor. Here fishermen, traders, and woodsmen mingled with residents of San Francisco and Virginia City who had summer cottages in this vicinity. The *Governor Blaisdel,* described as a "neat little ferry boat," ran between Tahoe City and the other lake community of Glenbrook, passing some steam-powered sawmills at the mouths of creeks on the western shore.

The only other settlements were the aforementioned south shore roadhouses for the Comstock traffic which was monitored by transportation and express companies. In the summer of 1864, one patient chronicler reported 6,667 men on foot alongside 883 horsemen, and more than 3,100 stagecoach trips by competing companies. By the time Nevada became a state in October 1864, five-year-old Virginia City, the destination of the silver-mad traffic, had several thousand inhabitants, the vast majority of whom were ex-Californians.

In late 1867, this road traffic slowed dramatically as the combination of the Central Pacific Railroad and stage traffic through the new town of Truckee provided even faster transportation between California and Nevada. But the lake would not enter into hibernation, for Virginia City's mining crowd was by this time making a serious bid to exploit Tahoe's lumber. The Comstock's enterprising shadow would soon creep upon the mountain lake's varied resources.

After the Comstock Lode experienced a successful mining revival early in the 1870s, ultimately resulting in the discovery of the fabulously rich, deep-lying "Big Bonanza" silver lode, Virginia City more than ever needed vast quantities of cut lumber and big timbers for the square-set supports which shored up miles of mine walls in the "city beneath the city." The Lake Tahoe Basin had virgin stands of timber in abundance, more than sufficient to satisfy the demand. Moreover, the Carson Range, a spur of the Sierra rimming the east side of Lake Tahoe, held numerous creeks and small lakes, all potential water sources. Noting these assets, Virginia Citians got busy.

WATER

Mine operators began to survey the region to determine the most expeditious way of conveying the water to the Comstock. The distance from the upper reaches of the watershed to reservoirs above Virginia City was 25 miles, but it involved a nearly 3,000-foot drop from the Carson Range to the Lakeview saddle in Washoe Valley before rising 1,700 to 1,800 feet to Virginia City. Initially, it was thought that expensive pumping works might be required to successfully transfer the water, but one German engineer noted the possible advantage of the gravity flow and devised a practical method of water transport, an inverted siphon that could withstand 800 pounds of pressure to the square inch, the equivalent of the perpendicular pressure of a 1,720-foot water column.

In 1871, the reorganized Virginia and Gold Hill Water Company constructed flumes and pieced together specially shaped pipes, each a foot in interior diameter, riveted together to withstand the intense pressure that the water fall would create. In all, about 700 tons of pipe were

GAIL BANDINI

▲ *The queen of the railroad short lines,* the Virginia & Truckee Railroad brought timber and supplies to the Comstock town from 1869 until well into the 20th century. Now restored, it operates as a tourist attraction throughout the summer.

used, each section having been specially manufactured at a San Francisco iron works and shipped to Lakeview by rail. Six weeks in its construction, the huge 38,300-foot-long pipeline could, after its completion in July 1873, successfully transport up to 2 million gallons daily.

When the first water flowed into Virginia City, the local *Territorial Enterprise* reported that its citizens were "as wild with joy as were the Israelites when Moses smote the rock to get water." All day long miners and others drank the sweet Tahoe water and watched its musical flow out of the flume. But the volume was insufficient and a second siphon had to be laid after the great Virginia City fire of 1875. After a third line from

▲ *Two hikers follow the water flume trail* hugging the hills high above Tahoe's Nevada shore. Along the path of a nearby east shore flume are the "bear slides," vertical erosion streaks that were created by overflow flume water. They suggest a playground for bears.

LARRY PROSOR

the Tahoe water basin was added in 1887, there was finally sufficient water to handle Virginia City's 6-million-gallon daily consumption, which also included adequate hydraulic power to generate electricity for various uses, especially to drive the huge Cornish pumps above the deep Comstock mine shafts.

TIMBER

At a 6,220-foot altitude in the desert Virginia Range, Virginia City had little access to trees for lumber, except for scattered scrubby pinyons which were soon consumed in the camp's early

years. But in extreme western Nevada along a 60-mile front of the eastern slope of the Sierra Nevada, from the Truckee River northeast of Lake Tahoe to the headwaters of the Carson River southeast of Lake Tahoe, pines stood in abundance at mile-high elevations and higher. In the 1860s these satisfied Virginia City's enormous appetite for wood, but eventually the heavily timbered sides of the Tahoe Basin itself and its stands of pine and fir would be systematically exploited by mining interests.

Thus until the early 1890s the forested mountains in the Lake Tahoe Basin saw intense logging and milling activity, adequately supplying Virginia City with lumber. Immense trees extended from Tahoe's west shoreline up the high-sloping mountainsides to the ever-present snow. Using a combination of axes and saws, brawny loggers felled the fir and pine, while horse, mule, and sometimes ox teams dragged the trimmed logs down to the sandy lake shore. On extremely steep hillsides log chutes were occasionally used in place of teams.

The wood, cut to manageable 16- to 40-foot lengths, was rolled into the deep-blue water, where a circle of long slim spars fastened together at each end with iron chains corraled the logs. The resulting boom adequately encircled the wedge-shaped raft which contained enough timber to make up to 300,000 feet of lumber. A strong cable connected the boom to small steamers which towed the load 12 to 20 miles eastward across Tahoe to hungry sawmills on the shores at Glenbrook, where during the height of the Comstock silver mining in the 1870s three major mills furiously cut wood.

Large wagons at first hauled the cut wood eastward from Glenbrook up a 6-mile stretch to Spooner's Summit, where wooden "V" flumes about 2 feet wide and 12 miles long sent the product at breakneck speed to vast wood yards located 2,000 feet below and a mile south of Carson City, where lumber trains of the Virginia and Truckee Railroad completed the delivery to the Comstock, 14 miles away. (After 1875, a 9-mile narrow-gage rail line expeditiously sent loads of cut boards and planks up the steep Glenbrook-Spooner's Summit grade.)

Here was industry of immense proportions, astonishing to the modern Tahoe visitor who sees only thick reforested mountainsides and modern high-rise resorts and recreation of all types. The demand for lumber was so great that government journalist Eliot Lord noted the Comstock's immense wood consumption in his official 1882 report. He declared that during 1874-1879 alone more than 300 million board feet of lumber had been delivered to Virginia City in addition to more than 1.1 million cords of wood for fuel. Lord also reported that over a 20-year period fully 600 million feet of lumber was shoring up mine tunnels, equivalent to enough wood to build houses for 150,000 people.

Three major companies cut and transported the lumber from forest to market. The Carson and Tahoe Lumber and Fluming Company, under the leadership of H. M. Yerington and Duane L. Bliss, for whom the large California state park north of Emerald Bay is named, built two logging railroads in the Camp Richardson area which brought up to 250,000 board feet daily to the long 1,800-foot wharf at Bijou. As many as 500 men worked for Bliss' company during peak summer operations. A second lumbering and fluming operation, the Sierra Nevada Wood and Lumber Company, owned a large mill on the Nevada Shore at Incline, a small railroad that ran to Sand Harbor, and its own flumes. A third company, Pacific Wood Lumber and Fluming, owned by Virginia City's largest mining operators, tapped northern Tahoe basin's timberlands.

An 1889 area guidebook described the bustling town of Truckee as being "in the center of a great and flourishing lumber industry." The cutting of timber and sawmilling continued well into the late 20th century. The last mill, the Louisiana-Pacific, immediately east of town, ▽ ceased operations in 1989.

"He who cannot content himself for a time at Tahoe, could not be satisfied in any place on earth...." 1880s Tourist Guide

Turn-of-the-Century Tahoe

While the sounds of logging and teaming filled the air and the sturdy trees on the steep mountainsides of Tahoe Basin were being systematically removed, another industry quickly developed for northern Californians and Nevadans—tourism. The construction of the transcontinental Central Pacific Railroad north of the Tahoe area early in 1868 led to the founding of the town of Truckee adjacent to Donner Lake as the new gateway to Tahoe. Though a rough lumbering town with 13 sawmills in the early 1870s, Truckee nevertheless maintained rules of etiquette. In the main hotel a posted notice read, "Gents are requested to wear their coats in the dining room."

The two-dollar stage trip from Truckee to the lake ran 15 delightful miles along pine forests and the rapid Truckee River, also utilized by lumbermen to float their logs to sawmills. Also en route was the setting of the Tahoe region's only mining

◀ **T**ahoe's north shore is set amid stands of green pine that descend from Mount Rose.

Though Lake ▶ Tahoe has more than 60 tributaries, it has only one outlet: through the wooden dam at the head of the Truckee River at Tahoe City.

GAIL BANDINI

▲ *Colorful rafters enjoy a blissful day on the Truckee River. The river's tributaries—Donner, Stampede, and Boca—provide rafting opportunities from the town of Truckee.*

activity at Knoxville which in the 1860s was touted as a "second Comstock." The stagecoach terminated at the Grand Central Hotel at Tahoe City which after 1871 became a popular resort for San Franciscans as well as mining people from Virginia City. This refurbished three-story hotel sported a cast-iron $800 kitchen range, shiny black walnut furniture, and Brussels carpets in every room. The Grand Central, where rooms rented for $20 a week per person, including three meals a day, was the principal Lake Tahoe hostelry until it burned in 1895.

At Tahoe City, hotel guests enjoyed boating, fishing, swimming, picnicking, hiking, rooms with fine views in every direction, comfortable carriage riding with spirited teams, or just loafing. Saloons served the choicest of liquors and the town's billiard parlor had separate tables for "gents" and ladies, in addition to some gaming.

Tahoe City quickly became the lake's largest community, but the older sawmilling town of Glenbrook on the Nevada side still had a few advantages. Tourists could ride to Spooner's Summit to view the discharge of lumber from the narrow-gage and its loading onto the great "V" flumes that sent the wood to Carson City. As the mountain railroad climbed the switchbacks, rumbled over a steep trestle and reversed itself high above the water's edge, sightseers were awed at every turn by grand, picturesque views of the lake. Back in Glenbrook, the billiard parlor boasted the best bowling alley in Nevada, and the hotel provided free rowboats for its guests.

HORACE GREELEY

Moreover, Glenbrook was often visited by the colorful, legendary Hank Monk, the stage driver who brought the noted New York newspaperman Horace Greeley (who originated the famous expression "Go West, Young Man!") to Lake Tahoe in a wild stage ride in 1859. As Monk took Greeley over breathless steep mountain passes and around cliffs with hairpin curves, he reassured his passenger by shouting "Keep your seat, Horace, we'll get you there on time!"

Greeley used this phrase and a picture of a stagecoach driven by six horses on his campaign posters when he ran for the Republican nomina-

Two-mile-long Emerald Bay contains ▶
Tahoe's only island, Fannette, long associated with "Captain Dick" Brater, an old 19th-century boatman, who was Emerald Bay's caretaker. In 1929, the ladies of nearby Vikingsholm Castle established a 16-square-foot teahouse atop the island, where the owner and her guests enjoyed afternoon teas.

tion for president in 1872. And, for years thereafter, a contemporary guidebook promised coach riders from Carson City to Glenbrook that "Hank Monk would be your Jehu and will land you safely at the Lake Shore House for dining and dancing."

Nevertheless, Tahoe City was the lake's headquarters for tourists and most boat excursions. From the local Custom House and its 600-foot wharf, regularly scheduled steamers sailed past smooth, pebble beaches and meadowed inlets. Going southerly, the first main stop was the family resort of McKinney's (today known as Chambers' Lodge).

The steamers next passed by Emerald Bay, a bright green-hued inlet which embraces Tahoe's only island. On it was a "tomb" excavated in the rock marked by a cross and a rude cabin built by Emerald Bay's owner, Ben Holladay, for his caretaker, the eccentric "Captain Dick" Brater. Captain Dick was later lost in a furious squall in another Tahoe inlet when his boat capsized, and so the old tar's body lies at the bottom of the lake instead of in the resting place readied for him on "Emerald Isle."

Only a few boat miles past Emerald Bay, at the south end of the lake in the shadow of 9,800-foot Mt. Tallac, was Yank's Hotel. Purchased by financier "Lucky" Baldwin after 1879, the name of the hotel was changed by the powerful developer to "Tallac House." Baldwin also acquired vast acres of cedar and pine which even today contain the largest stands of virgin timber along Tahoe's shores. In 1883, lessees made significant improvements including bridle paths, roads and trails, bathhouses and rebuilt dwellings, and the wharf. With its fishing and boating, Tallac soon became the lake's most elegant resort, enjoying the top distinction until 1900.

Advertisements of the era boasted that vacationing at the clear-water lake and admiring its beauties would bring ultimate satisfaction and even improvements in health and disposition. George Crofutt's annual tourist guides of the 1870s and 1880s urged its readers to come to

Tahoe for a time. "When once there, sailing on the beautiful lake, gazing far down its shining, pebbly bottom, hooking the sparkling trout that makes the pole sway and bend in your hand like a willow wand, you will be in no hurry to leave. If you become tired of sailing and angling, take your gun and tramp into the hills and fill your game pouch with quail and grouse, and perhaps you might come upon a deer or bear. He who cannot content himself for a time at Tahoe, could not be satisfied in any place on earth, he would need to find a new and better world."

Indeed, the highly-sought-after cutthroat trout weighed up to 20 pounds, and occasionally an astonishing 26 pounds! To handle the fried,

Overleaf: *Stands of sturdy pines* ▶
frame Emerald Bay backed by Nevada's Carson Range. Photo by Jeff Gnass.

◄ *Fallen Leaf Lake, a two-mile-long and* one-mile-wide sheet of water, is separated from Emerald Bay by an ancient glacial hump. It empties into Lake Tahoe by way of a small stream. Stanford Camp is situated on the shore.

baked, or broiled brown trout is "not bad employment for the jaws to masticate the crisp, juicy morsels—it is not bad *jawing*," according to one correspondent. But by century's end commercial fishing cut down on available fish, and the extensive sawmilling and logging operations on spawning creeks had contaminated water sources with wood chips, sawdust, and other residue left behind by woodsmen. As the densely wooded mountainsides had been gradually denuded to supply both railroad and mining interests, Lake Tahoe became a somewhat less glamorous place to visit by the turn of the century.

THE 20TH CENTURY

At the dawn of the 20th century, the extensive logging operations at Lake Tahoe had forever passed out of the picture in favor of an economy firmly based on recreation and tourism. This shift is amply exemplified by the completion in 1900 of a new 15-mile railway from Truckee, located on the mainline Central Pacific, to Tahoe City. From the onset the iron horses tooted not for lumbermen but for the benefit of tourists, who jammed Tahoe City's busy hotels during the summer season of early June to mid-September. As a further demonstration of the economic shift, the logging railroad at Glenbrook was dismantled and barged across the lake to Tahoe City, where the entire rolling stock and other equipment was integrated into the new line.

Also in 1900, the old Hot Springs Hotel east of Tahoe City became Brockway under aggressive new ownership. A new resort opened in 1903 at Fallen Leaf, soon followed by others at Homewood, Meeks Bay, and Tahoe Pines. But it would be the stylish, gabled-roofed, three-story Tahoe Tavern, located immediately south of Tahoe City, that would thereafter be the pacesetter and headquarters for Tahoe excursionists and vacationers.

Built in 1901, the magnificently landscaped Tahoe Tavern, with its distinctive ornate wood facade, experienced additions over the years, including a casino in 1907. It was practically a city-style hotel with a large high-ceilinged ballroom, bowling alley, laundry, and barber shop. No other Tahoe Basin hotel had such appointments, and Tahoe Tavern with its own railway station received guests at its doorstep well into the 1930s. The magnificent 650-foot transportation pier served the lake steamers that plied between other Tahoe communities and small resorts.

It was at Tahoe Tavern that the noted California travel author George Wharton James penned his well-received book *Lake of the Sky* in 1914. He noted that at this luxurious resort, the comfort-conscious set mingled with sportsmen, swimmers, and hikers. "It is not a fashionable resort in the sense that everyone, men and women alike, must dress in fashionable garb to be welcomed and made at home," reported James. "If one comes in from a hunting or a fishing trip at dinner time, he is expected to enter the dining room as he is." In the casino and in the dining room folk in white flannels rubbed shoulders with people of means in conventional evening dress. The management urged guests to bring old clothes to wear while hiking, riding, boating, fishing, horseback riding, and strolling in the woods to gather flowers. But the tavern epitomized opulence as well, and the higher society enjoyed the comforts of good cuisine, popular dance bands, and a swimming pool surrounded by sun decks. The resort is no more—it was torn down and today the site is just one condominium development among many.

The rails were not the only way to reach Tahoe's charm. Automobiles kicking up dust trails traversed the Sierra Nevada roller-coaster highways from Sacramento, California (now Interstate 80 and U.S. 50). Pre-World War I travelers used both routes in coming and going to Tahoe following a 260-mile wishbone pattern, with each leg of the breathtaking journey following old emigrant trails which by this time were 30 years old. The "modern" highways were pot-holed, dusty country roads that darted around trees and rocky crags, hugging the hillsides. Still, summertime travelers from Sacramento could

reach Tahoe in a day; inclement weather and snow made the roads at times impassable during the winter.

The most picturesque part of the wishbone route was the 26-mile distance between Tahoe City and Tallac, now known as West Lake Drive. Daily stages using old-time convertible automobiles with running boards and narrow tires ran beside summer homes, rocky cliffs, and sections of second-growth timber. Every turn brought the visitor new views of the placid blue lake on one hand or snowy summits reaching into still deeper blue in the sky.

One June day in 1914, an ecstatic reporter motoring on the West Shore Road remarked about the sheer delight and surprises encountered along the route:

> Up and down we glide, the soft purring of the motor as we run on the level changing to the chug-chugging of the up-pulls, or the grip of the brake as we descend. Every few feet new vistas of beauty are projected before us. The moving pictures are all exquisite. Indeed, after many studies of this incomparable Lake Tahoe I verily believe there is no

A *featured attraction for visitors of Tallac Historic Site is the Baldwin House, built as a residence on* land owned by "Lucky" Baldwin, a 19th-century entrepreneur. He accumulated hundreds of acres between this site southward to the present Tahoe Keys. He converted a small hotel into the first-class Tallac House, ▽ *dubbed the "Saratoga of the Pacific," whose site is just a few hundred yards away.*

more beautiful spot on it than Meeks Bay seen from this road.

To get its full charm we stop the machine for a while. Looking back we discover that the curve where we rest is a marvelous outlook point. We have ascended to a good height and look down upon the Lake. There are light blue, emerald green, deep blue in patches and in long irregularly shaped points. Here are Como, Maggiore, Lugano and Windermere all in one, though as yet free from the houses and artificial gardens on the slopes. But nature such as this needs none of man's adornment to make it perfect....

Today there are a score or more of fishermen out in their little boats, and strange to say, all of them near enough to be seen, are fishing in a patch of deep blue. The water there must be deeper than elsewhere, for there is where they invariably get their best catches.

Now we come to the wild and rugged scenery. We are hemmed in on the right by towering crags and walls of massive gray rock. Shattered and seamed, scarred and disintegrated, they look as though earthquake and lightning shock and the storms of a thousand years had battled with them. They give a new touch of grandeur and almost awesome sublimity to the scene.

For a mile or two we play at hide and seek with the Lake. ...It seems as though we were in the hands of a wizard. "Now you see it, now you don't." ...Query: "Where is the Lake?" Mountains, snowbanks, granite walls, trees galore, creeks flashing their white crests dashing down their stony courses toward the Lake, but only now and then do we catch fleeting glimpses of it. All at once it bursts full and clear again upon our enraptured vision, but only to give us a full taste of its supernal beauty before we are whirled around a curve where the eye rests upon nothing but the rugged majesty of the Sierras.

Now we curve around high up above Emerald Bay, that small glacial lake, the eastern terminal moraine of which was unfortunately torn through, so that the "lake" disappeared and became a "bay" of the great Lake itself. Every moment of this portion of the ride is a delight. The senses are kept keenly alert, for not only have we the Lake, the bay and the mountains, but part of the way we have flowers and shrubs by the thousands, bees and butterflies flit to and fro, and singing streams come foaming white from the snowbanks above, eager to reach the Lake.... Now Mt. Tallac, in all his serene majesty, looms ahead. Snow a hundred or more feet deep in places covers his rocky sides....

Below us is the emerald-ringed bay, with its romantic little island at the west end, and nearby the joyously-shouting Eagle Creek as it plunges over the precipice and makes the foam-flecked Eagle Falls.

INTEREST RISES IN TAHOE'S WATER

It was not merely tourists' eyes that were looking with great interest at Lake Tahoe. Rapidly growing northern California looked for new water sources for domestic and industrial use and to generate power, and Nevada's Senator Francis Newlands sought to develop agriculture in western Nevada through federal reclamation projects. The question, then, was how to develop these multiple uses without materially affecting the lake's water level.

▲ *A* short hike from Emerald Bay, Lower *Eagle Falls cascades from crystal-clear pools in a picturesque tree-studded canyon, tumbling 1,500 feet toward Vikingsholm Castle.*

◀ *A*s viewed from high above Lake *Tahoe, the breathtaking inlet Emerald Bay is bound by a rugged brace of rocky mountains informally known as the "back fence."*

29

▲ *Several cruise boats, including the "Sunrunner," sail alongside their larger counterparts, such as the "M.S. Dixie" and the "Tahoe Queen." All operate daily during the summer months, though larger boats offer climate-controlled comfort and are available year-round.*

Prior to 1900 some water disputes flared among private concerns involving all levels of government. But when Senator Newlands devised a new plan to employ Lake Tahoe water to reclaim western Nevada desert lands in 1902, interest rose anew as to how to appropriate water between various California and Nevada interests. Clarification of rights of various claimants was sorely needed.

For the next 17 years various governmental agencies and private interest groups tried to hammer out joint efforts toward the use of Tahoe water. But most new arrangements failed to satisfy anybody, leaving only more questions. Who would actually control the lake's water level?

Who would own the water lapping up to the lake's shorelines? Who could claim the water flowing on the Truckee River? In 1919, Lake Tahoe's level fell well below 6,223 feet, further aggravating all parties.

In 1924, the head of the U.S. Reclamation Service, Elwood Mead, negotiated a new agreement by which the Reclamation Service could pump up to 300 cubic feet a second during the growing season to irrigate 87,500 acres in Nevada, if the present lake level could be maintained. Amendments to the agreement were made over the next several years, each trying to patch the fragile truce between the states. Finally in 1934, after much deliberating, new specifications were promulgated calling for a lake level never lower than 6,223 feet and a maximum high level of 6,229.1 feet.

At low levels the Secretary of the Interior would have to approve pumping for irrigation in Nevada or for sanitary or domestic purposes in either state. The new agreement allowed for the construction of Boca Dam and Reservoir on the Truckee River at its confluence with the Little Truckee. Completed in 1939, the new reservoir greatly reduced the necessity of always looking to Lake Tahoe for water. A reclarification in 1944 affirmed water rights for the Pyramid Lake Paiute Indians in Nevada.

▲ **H**igh in the lofty Sierra at a 9,000-foot *altitude and above the obscuring mists at Heavenly Valley, snow has covered the pines and frosted the hillsides.*

Colorful hues and glinting skies of *autumn along the Truckee River offer visitors opportunities for change-of-season* ▽ *hiking and fishing.*

LARRY PROSOR

A decade later, in 1955, an interstate compact made further significant modifications, including addressing the problem of sewage and the amount of fresh water pumped from Lake Tahoe Basin. As the 20th century wore on, disputes continued to rage over the fair apportionment of the precious water among Nevada's agricultural interests, the Pyramid Indians, commercial users in Reno and Sparks, and eastern California entities.

Finally in December 1990, Congress pushed through a far-reaching bill which settled numerous long-standing lawsuits. Fully 90 percent of the Truckee River water would go to Nevada and the remainder to California. Water conservation measures in Reno and Sparks would be implemented, and the U.S. Interior Department would manage the 7,520-acre Stillwater National Wildlife Refuge east of Fallon in Lahontan Valley. In the settlement the Pyramid Lake Paiute Tribe gained money for economic development and a fishing fund.

Lake Tahoe's high-rise hotels definitely add to the image of the south shore as being "Los Angeles in the Pines."

Lake Tahoe's Modern Era

Although Lake Tahoe's modern era began immediately after World War II, the completion in 1938 of the all-weather road encircling the lake stands out as most important in preparing the area for rapid, post-war growth. This truly excellent highway ultimately led to the elimination of the once busy Tahoe steamers and also the disappearance of the old work-horse, the Lake Tahoe Railway. Until it ceased operations in 1943, that famous shortline served as a major tourist carrier from Truckee southward to Tahoe Tavern, a classic turn-of-the-century resort. Just south of Tahoe City, passengers disembarked from the railway could, at the end of a long pier, make convenient steamer connections to other lake resorts.

The initial post-war growth began at the lake's south

◀ **Challenged by the** extreme terrain, a Tahoe skier races across the white rooftop of a steep Sierra ski slope.

Formerly a grotto ▷ 70 feet into the mountainside, and believed by area Washoe Indians to be inhabited by demons, Cave Rock is now tunneled through by U.S. 50.

GAIL BANDINI

▲ *Jutting up among the pines, Nevada's south shore hotels at Stateline provide continuous* *entertainment. In winter, except for brave boaters and fishermen, the cold, blue Tahoe waters are generally* *forsaken in favor of skiing at nearby Heavenly Valley and about 15 other area facilities. The rugged* *snow-clad Sierra Nevada looms in the background.*

shore. Although this area boasted only about 1,000 year-round residents in the mid-1940s, promoters eager for tourist dollars soon brought rapid changes. Along the south shore, the popular European sport of downhill skiing quickly caught on, and various businessmen opened small motels, cafes, and gift shops to handle the burgeoning crowds.

By 1950, the combined south-shore communities of Al Tahoe, Bijou, and Stateline had experienced a tripling of population. Gambling on the Nevada side of the line was still confined to a few slot machines in the restaurants and a table game or two in the saloons. By 1954, however, the original six-stool cafe known as Harvey's had expanded into a full-fledged modern hotel-casino. Today, Harvey's Wagon Wheel is an impressive, multistoried enterprise occupying a sixth of a mile of highway frontage on U.S. 50.

Directly across the street, William Harrah, who pioneered the creation of the modern, efficient, corporate-style gambling casino, soon constructed one of the most elaborate and highly regarded Nevada hotel-casinos. Its shares were publicly offered and for years Harrah's was Nevada's only five-star hotel. With other small saloons and gambling clubs nearby, the half-mile of U.S. 50 abutting the California state line became the lake's smaller version of the Las Vegas Strip. Weekend casino players now joined winter skiers in flocking to the lake, instead of nearby Reno, and by 1965 the south shore population approached 14,000.

In that same year, all of the California south-shore communities incorporated to form the new city of South Lake Tahoe. More than 25 years later, in the early 1990s, this city of 30,000 was the scene of an ambitious redevelopment plan which saw the removal of almost all of the older motels, street reroutings, construction of modern residential and commercial buildings, and the creation of designated bike paths and a large pedestrian plaza. South Lake Tahoe is perhaps most famous for the Heavenly Valley ski resort and the wall-

▲ *Squaw Valley gained international fame when the 1960 Winter Olympic Games were staged here. In addition to world-class skiing, the valley offers summer visitors scenic beauty and a variety of recreational opportunities including high Sierra views from the cable-car tramway.*

to-wall motels, where "plungers" can catch a few catnaps before resuming their affair with Lady Luck.

For several years the adjacent Nevada gambling community of Stateline has tried to change its name, for obvious commercial reasons, to simply Lake Tahoe. Its three high-rise hotels definitely add to the image of the south shore as being "Los Angeles in the Pines," but its pleasure seekers are mostly from the Bay Area and Sacramento.

Auto tourists driving north from Lake Tahoe, Nevada, on the 72-mile drive around the lake first encounter the small communities of Round Hill, Zephyr Cove, Marla Bay, and Cave Rock. The famous Glenbrook, once renowned for its lumber mills in the 1860s, is now a posh residential community containing some of Nevada's most expensive non-commercial real estate.

▶ Besides government-operated campgrounds along the Truckee River, private facilities such as Meeks Bay Resort on the lake itself offer seclusion for vacationers who seek to escape the crowds.

The conservative ▷ setting of the north shore's Cal-Neva Hotel at Crystal Bay belies a raffish past. Born amid the "Roaring Twenties," the then motel-bar was a stylish speakeasy. Various owners after World War II kept the doors open between government-forced closings. Now the respectable Cal-Neva is the community's commercial mainstay.

GAIL BANDINI

TOURIST ATTRACTIONS

After turning north from U.S. 50, just before Spooner's Summit, tourists drive on Highway 28 to the north-shore community of Incline Village. The Ponderosa Ranch of television's *Bonanza* fame is a major tourist attraction, and the modern Hyatt Regency Hotel-Casino emerges amid the pines and mountain scenery. Proceeding west along the north shore, Crystal Bay is next encountered. It is the home of the famous Cal-Neva Lodge, the lake's oldest gaming resort, once owned by entertainer Frank Sinatra. Nevada's north shore ends just a mile or so west of the state line.

California's northwest shore is dominated by Tahoe City, a town that is a world removed from the bustle of South Lake Tahoe. Everything can be found here for the summertime sportsman including excellent modern accommodations, restaurants, supermarkets, and specialty shops. East of Tahoe City are the alpine communities of Lake Forest, Cedar Flat, Carnelian Bay, Tahoe Vista, Kings Beach, and Brockway. South of Tahoe City, in more remote settings on Highway

89, are Sunnyside, Tahoe Pines, Homewood, Chambers Landing, Tahoma, Meeks Bay, and Rubicon Bay. Interspersed among Tahoe's small communities are natural wetlands, state parks, federal campgrounds, beautiful stretches of private land, public beaches, and rocky cliffs that fall directly into clean blue water.

Still further south, Emerald Bay is generally conceded to be the most beautiful location in all the Tahoe Basin. Located 17 miles south of Tahoe City, its picturesque island with small teahouse and the classic Vikingsholm Castle are world famous. After leaving Emerald Bay and traversing a narrow section of road, it is only a short distance to Camp Richardson and just a few miles further to complete the 72-mile trip around the lake through South Lake Tahoe and back to the gambling district at Stateline.

PRESERVING THE ENVIRONMENT

Although efforts to preserve and protect Lake Tahoe began prior to 1920, it was only the urbanization of the area in the 1950s and '60s, with the resulting vast changes, that made the

***N**ow part of* ▷ *California's Emerald Bay State Park, Vikingsholm Castle was built and furnished in 1929 at a cost of about $500,000. Among the finest examples of Scandinavian architecture built in the New World, the castle faithfully reproduces a 9th-century Norse fortress and contains 38 rooms.*

GAIL BANDINI

***A** street of false-fronted buildings serves as a backdrop for simulated gunfights, just one of many attractions at the Ponderosa Ranch, located on a hillside setting on Tahoe's northeast shore. Here is the legendary home of TV's* ▽ *"Bonanza" series.*

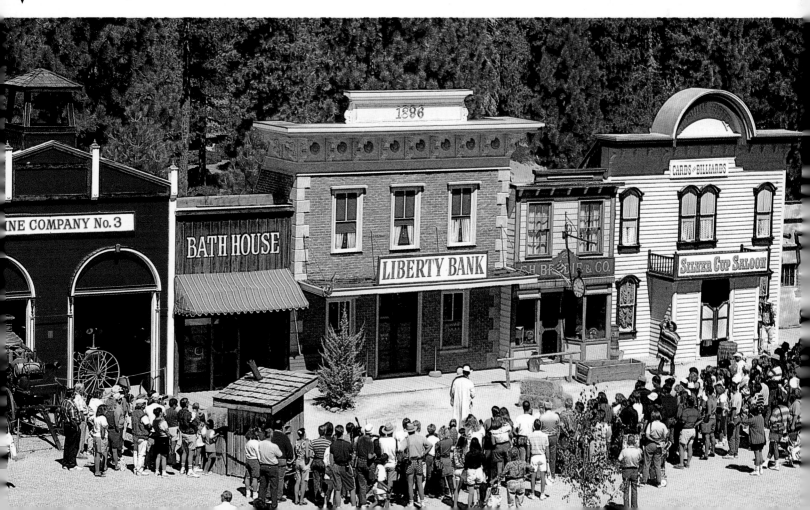

▲ *The Taylor Creek Visitor Center, operated by the USDA Forest Service, offers* an exhibit hall, nature trails, and the Stream Profile Chamber where visitors may see native Kokanee trout in their natural setting through underwater panels.

residents conscious of preserving the environment. Major concerns included were loss of much of the former open shoreline space to private land development, encroachment of housing developments on critical and fragile areas, loss of water purity and clarity with increased algae growth, air pollution, and traffic congestion.

These worries eventually led to the 1969 creation of the Tahoe Regional Planning Agency (TRPA). It took congressional action to create this organization which from its inception exercised greater authority than any of the local governments within the five counties with Tahoe shorelines: Placer and El Dorado counties in California, and Carson City, Washoe, and Douglas counties in Nevada. The 15-member agency exerts kingly rule in establishing environmental standards and enforcing regional plans and ordinances to achieve orderly change and development.

With a stated goal of expanding public land ownership in the Tahoe Basin to about 85 percent, during the 1970s the federal government earnestly began to acquire sections of private Tahoe property. Administered by the Lake Tahoe Basin Management Unit, an operating arm of the Forest Service, the government purchased the historic middle-class resorts of Meeks Bay, Camp Richardson, and Zephyr Cove. "Lucky" Baldwin's Tallac estate, near Camp Richardson, also came under Forest Service jurisdiction.

The Lake Tahoe Basin Management Unit normally leases their acquired facilities to concessionaires, officially designated as permittees. America's largest ski resort, Heavenly Valley, was among the early lessees, signing their first agreement on April 19, 1954. Permittees operate with close government supervision, under an ecological umbrella that generally discourages new commercialization and seeks to maintain, rather than increase, existing levels of service and development. A notable exception is the recent trend to make virtually all public facilities more readily available to the physically handicapped. This promises to be a dominant issue between small businessmen and various government entities until well into the next century.

TAHOE'S CHANGING SEASONS

For many of the Lake Tahoe Basin's 65,000 permanent residents, the passing of summer comes as a welcome change from the July and August period of intense tourist activity. The summer commercial season usually ends with Labor Day in early September as vacationers retreat to warmer localities and second-home families return to meet the start of a new school year. Although the casinos still draw good crowds until November, small business operators now find relief from the influx of summer "flatlanders" and they attempt to regroup and adjust to the slower pace of life.

As snow flurries can arrive as early as September, local residents look ahead to winter. It is time to drop dead trees, bring in extra supplies, and buck, split, and stack large quantities of pine, cedar, and fir for firewood for the inevitable onset of cold weather. It is also time to install snow tires, and for locals without four-wheel-drive vehicles to make certain that all the links in the tire chains are solid.

By early fall, many businesses and the majority of campgrounds are closed. Tourists arriving late in September sometimes feel out of place, occasionally inquiring about the Tahoe crowds that they had heard so much about. Probably as many as 80 percent of the cabins (even higher percentages on the west shore) stand deserted from mid-September through mid-May. These residences

Ehrman Mansion, a turn-of-the-century Tahoe social center, can be toured during the summer season.

In the Tahoe ▷ Keys Marina, a part of the city of South Lake Tahoe, pleasure boats of all sizes and shapes find safe harbor amid narrow channels. Alongside the water rise attractive homes.

▲ *Youthful exuberance is depicted by these downhill ski enthusiasts who have just executed a difficult turn on a Tahoe ski slope. Ski races are just part of the varied program at North Star.*

serve primarily as seasonal summer vacation homes and most were not constructed for winter usage. Anti-freeze becomes a much-desired commodity as water pipes are drained and the protective oily liquid is poured down kitchen and bathroom fixtures.

With the loss of tourist dollars, local businessmen find their checkbook balances on the decline. They know, however, that now is the time to take care of all the maintenance and repairs that were neglected during the hectic summer.

October's coolness and winds are often delightfully interrupted by Indian Summer, the rekindling of early August weather amidst the changing colors of autumn. The warm, soft air suggests the season's final boat excursion, a last opportunity for a steak barbecue on a stretch of sandy beach, or just quietly relaxing, watching the chipmunks and birds scurry feverishly in search of provisions for the upcoming winter. The respite never lasts, however. Suddenly and without warning comes a quick frost followed by the first in a long string of light recurring snow flurries.

WINTER ARRIVES

Winter arrives in mid-December, but to the surprise of many visitors, Tahoe more often than not fails to experience a white Christmas. Many small storms pass through the Tahoe Basin throughout December and January without anyone giving them a second thought. Although Tahoe witnessed extreme drought conditions throughout the last half of the 1980s and into the early 1990s, each winter the lakeside communities can usually count on a few large two- to three-foot snowfalls, each occurring over a short period of a day or so.

When the satellite weather system forecasts an advancing front and winter storm warnings are posted, a sense of excitement seizes the local population. First comes the ominous word of a Pacific low-pressure area advancing toward the California coast and storm warnings are announced along the 450-mile ocean front from Cape Mendocino southward to Point Conception. Heavy rains sweep inland, first reaching San Francisco and the Bay, then moving into Sacramento and other central valley communities before then striking the low elevations on the west side of the Sierra. In the Tahoe Basin temperatures begin to dip, but the first precipitation is usually mere rain and not snow. The clouds grow darker and the barometer falls. Grocery stores and supermarkets are full of locals and tourists scrambling to stock up on essentials before driving gets difficult.

As snow begins to accumulate on the roadways, it is easy to determine who is prepared for the storm. Drivers without chains get stuck in

LARRY PROSOR

▲ *Two skiers momentarily halt on their*
way along a Heavenly Valley ski trail.

◄ *The chair lift at Tahoe's Ski Bowl*
seemingly drops the skiers into the
deep-blue waters of the "foot-bathing
pool of the Gods."

snowdrifts after short slides off the roads. Batteries which turned engines over easily at warm, sea-level elevations oftentimes fail in below freezing climates, and drivers sit concerned as their ignition only grinds away. Cars seem to be having problems everywhere. Wind-blown snow greatly reduces visibility and small boulders and tree limbs fall on the highways. Wipers barely keep windshields clean, and tire chains are so full of snow that the familiar click-click-click almost disappears in the eerie silence of white.

Soon the snow is falling so fast that the plows are now behind in their vain attempts to keep the highways bladed. Bright flares guide still-mobile cars around a wreck or a vehicle partially off the road. Tow trucks are unable to reach stranded motorists. Not long afterwards, roads

begin to close—the first is usually Highway 89 in the Emerald Bay area. All traffic is halted and soon travel anywhere around the lake is impossible. In severe storms, Donner Summit on Interstate 80 and Echo Summit on U.S. 50 also close, thereby shutting down two major cross-country arterials and stranding long lines of trucks attempting to climb both sides of the Sierra.

Carefree skiers in their brightly colored gear reluctantly seek refuge in the lodges and cafes. Snow is heavy on car roofs, with restaurants and saloons jammed with coffee drinkers, all asking "How much snow will we get?" and "When will there be a break in the weather?"

The snow does recede within a day or two, and the great storm dies. Ski resort operators now wear the biggest smiles, while crowds on

◄ ▲ Fishing at Tahoe and in the nearby Truckee River is a popular pastime. During spawning season salmon are found in the clear water of a feeder creek.

the slopes whoop it up. Everywhere is snow, snow, snow. All make it their business to move the white, fluffy stuff. Stores and shops resume regular hours and schools, which may have closed their doors for a day or two, now reopen. Residents shovel snow off driveways, highway crews with snowplows work to widen driveable road areas, and sand and salt are thrown everywhere. It is a grand and glorious time for all!

Temperatures occasionally drop to zero at lake level, but Tahoe itself never freezes over because of its great depth, which averages 500 to 1,000 feet, reaching 1,645 feet near the northern shore. Bays and creeks routinely freeze, failing to have the depth advantage.

The first heavy winter storms bring much enthusiasm and excitement, but when they continue on and on into mid and late spring, they dash hopes and dreams of warmer days and an early summer. Despondency fills the air. "Well,

here we go again!" becomes a common greeting among the locals.

During the very short spring season, snow remains on the ground at lake level through May, and scattered snow flurries occur as late as mid-June. In early May, many Tahoe businessmen begin to seriously plan for the summer, inventorying their stock and ordering goods for what must be America's shortest business season. They join with the locals and the wise Solomon, "For lo! the winter is past, the snow is over and gone; the flowers appear on the earth and the time of the singing of birds is come...."

THE MAGIC OF SUMMER

Tahoe visitors during the magic time of summer, who avoid the lake during other seasons, carry away with them only an idyllic portrait of warm sandy beaches and delightfully cool evenings. From mid-June to Labor Day, the tradi-

The beaches at Sand Harbor State Park are enjoyed by those seeking the sun's browning rays, occasionally cooled by the waft of a Tahoe breeze. After too much of a good thing, ▼ there is plentiful shade to retreat into.

▲ *In years gone by stern-wheeler races, reminiscent of those on the flatlands of the Mississippi River, were reenacted at a 6,175-foot mountain-studded altitude on serene waters between the south shore and Emerald Bay. Today, these colorful races are but a memory.*

tional vacation period for public school in California, tourists arrive in waves and the sounds of summer are everywhere.

A variety of water activities meet every need. There are the traditional activities of swimming, scuba-diving, and fishing. While adults patiently seek out the Mackinaw and Kokanee, their children hunt for crayfish among the rocks and jetties.

Probably the best way to see the lake is on the large stern-wheel paddleboats which regularly ply from South Lake Tahoe and Zephyr Cove to Emerald Bay. Local resorts also rent jet skis, speedboats, and party barges for those eager to brave Tahoe's choppy water on their own. Windsurfing became a popular lake activity in the 1980s, and the more adventurous try parasailing high above the waves. Rubber rafting on the Truckee River, from Tahoe City downstream to the River Ranch, is an activity that tourists should not miss.

Camping is a favorite lake activity with two

dozen facilities available, ranging from no hookups to full service with water, sewer, and electricity. Campgrounds surround the lake, but the west shore is the predominant location as it contains the greatest number of state and federal campgrounds. Most summer visitors take one or more hiking excursions on well-maintained trails. In order of popularity, they are the one-mile hike up from Emerald Bay to Eagle Lake, and the nearly four-mile hike from Meeks Bay to Lake Genevieve. For the experienced hiker, the unfinished 150-mile Tahoe Rim Trail encircles the Lake Tahoe Basin at mountain crest altitudes.

A *forest ranger escorts nature lovers* ▷
along a Tahoe footpath explaining the surroundings, the flora and the fauna.

▲ *A windsurfer "catches some air." This popular aquatic sport dates back to Virginia City's heyday.*

Horseback riding is a favorite summer activity, with an excellent rental stable located adjacent to Camp Richardson. Many bicycle enthusiasts attempt the 72-mile trip around the lake, although the bike trail is not as yet complete and there are significant stretches where it is necessary to ride on the main highway. Bike rental opportunities are common, but many vacationers bring their own favorite two-wheelers. It is hard to conceive of an activity that is not done at Lake Tahoe. From bird-watching to hang gliding, from insect collecting to bungee-cord jumping, tennis, golf, bowling—it is all somewhere in the Tahoe Basin.

Distinct from the traditional cookstove and tent crowd who rough it at Yosemite or Yellowstone are the modern Tahoe campers, who might rent a kayak or lie on the beach until the late afternoon chill sends them back to their cabin or travel trailer for a short rest and a shower. These urbanites then change into sport coats and dresses and venture out for the evening to the saloons and the night life at Tahoe's Nevada casinos. Then it is back to "camp" for a night's sleep before another fast-paced day at the lake.

Gambling fever reaches a high point during the summer months. Slot machines keyed to multi-million-dollar jackpots excite Californians who are prohibited from playing back home. Sports betting has become very popular in recent years and baseball attracts much support during the summer. For great food and the best in live entertainment, the hotel-casinos on the south shore are difficult to beat.

*E*very conceivable water sport is available *at Lake Tahoe. In executing a wide turn, this enthusiastic water skier creates a long*
▽ *"rooster tail."*

Versatile Tahoe indeed has something for everybody along its 71 miles of shoreline and 193 square miles of surface area. The grandeur-filled rugged Sierra stretches most of the length of California embracing dozens of alpine lakes and countless streams. But nowhere does the majesty and charm of the Sierras' natural features combine better than at Lake Tahoe—a lake that is "millions of years deep."

SUGGESTED READING

HINKLE, GEORGE. *Sierra-Nevada Lakes.* Reno: University of Nevada Press, 1987.

JAMES, GEORGE WHARTON. *Lake of the Sky.* Reno: Nevada Publications, 1991 (originally printed in 1915).

SCOTT, EDWARD B. *The Saga of Lake Tahoe.* [2 volumes] Crystal Bay, Nevada: Sierra-Tahoe Publ. Co., 1957, 1973.

VAN ETTEN, CAROL. *Meeks Bay Memories.* Reno, Nevada: Silver Syndicate Press, 1994.

LARRY PROSOR

▲ **T**wo sailboats, with spinnakers unfurled, move leisurely along Tahoe's surface on a late afternoon cruise.

The Incline Village 18-hole public golf course, one of five such facilities
▼ around the lake, is situated in a pine forest that trails toward the lake.

The summer pace at Lake Tahoe slows toward day's end when even the most active sportsmen pay homage to the important hush of the sunset, as did this 1882 visitor from Oakland:

No painter would ever dare to put upon canvass the variegated colors of Tahoe's waters in a summer sunset. ...None but those who have witnessed the scene could be persuaded of its reality. Such beauty could not be, were it not for the highly reflective qualities of the pure translucent waters, which serve as a polished mirror of French plate glass.

First is reflected the delicate, gauzy, pearly-gray haze which surrounds the mountain boundaries...and which forms the groundwork of the glorious picture. Later, this shades off into violet; and, as the sun sinks, the mountains take on the most delicious crimson flush, deepening into purple. All of this beauty is reflected upon the surface of the lake. Here stretches out a shadow like...a deep band of crimson; again, further on, a deep purple, shaded at the edges with blue and green. These streamers of beautiful light and shade stretch far across the lake....

Edwards' Tourist Guide

◀ Nestled in a forested, mountain-rimmed setting, Lake Tahoe-Nevada State Park draws lovers of natural scenery to North America's largest alpine lake.

JEFF GNASS

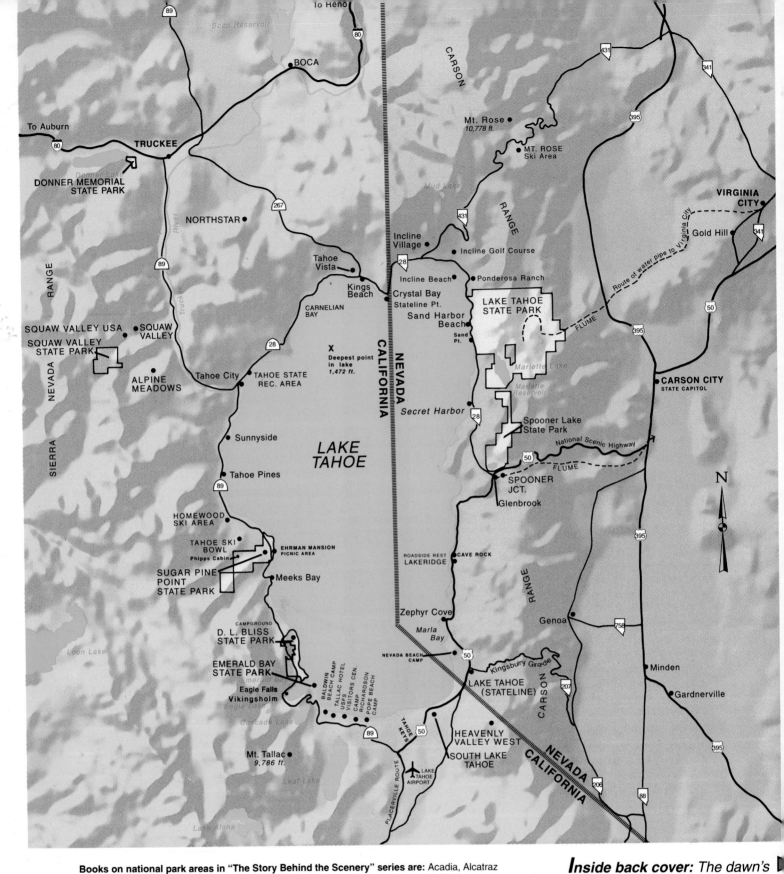

Books on national park areas in "The Story Behind the Scenery" series are: Acadia, Alcatraz Island, Arches, Big Bend, Biscayne, Blue Ridge Parkway, Bryce Canyon, Canyon de Chelly, Canyonlands, Cape Cod, Capitol Reef, Channel Islands, Civil War Parks, Colonial, Crater Lake, Death Valley, Denali, Devils Tower, Dinosaur, Everglades, Fort Clatsop, Gettysburg, Glacier, Glen Canyon-Lake Powell, Grand Canyon, Grand Canyon-North Rim, Grand Teton, Great Basin, Great Smoky Mountains, Haleakala, Hawaii Volcanoes, Independence, Lake Mead-Hoover Dam, Lassen Volcanic, Lincoln Parks, Mammoth Cave, Mesa Verde, Mount Rainier, Mount Rushmore, National Park Service, National Seashores, North Cascades, Olympic, Petrified Forest, Redwood, Rocky Mountain, Scotty's Castle, Sequoia & Kings Canyon, Shenandoah, Statue of Liberty, Theodore Roosevelt, Virgin Islands, Yellowstone, Yosemite, Zion.

Additional books in "The Story Behind the Scenery" series are: Annapolis, Big Sur, California Gold Country, California Trail, Colorado Plateau, Columbia River Gorge, Fire: A Force of Nature, Grand Circle Adventure, John Wesley Powell, Kauai, Lake Tahoe, Las Vegas, Lewis & Clark, Monument Valley, Mormon Temple Square, Mormon Trail, Mount St. Helens, Nevada's Red Rock Canyon, Nevada's Valley of Fire, Oregon Trail, Oregon Trail Center, Santa Catalina, Santa Fe Trail, Sharks, Sonoran Desert, U.S. Virgin Islands, Water: A Gift of Nature, Whales.

Call (800-626-9673), fax (702-433-3420), or write to the address below.

Published by KC Publications, 3245 E. Patrick Ln., Suite A, Las Vegas, NV 89120.

Inside back cover: *The dawn's radiant light sets Emerald Bay aglow w a riot of colors. Photo by Larry Ulri*

Created, Designed and Published in the U.S.A
Printed by Dong-A Publishing and Printing, Seoul, Korea
Color Separations by Kedia/Kwangyangsa Co., Ltd